FAKE NEWS
FAKE PRESIDENT

STEFANO FUGAZZI

FAKE NEWS
FAKE PRESIDENT

ABC ECONOMICS

abceconomics.com

ABC Economics is committed to a sustainable future for our readers and our planet.

Book design by abceconomics.com
Cover picture by Stefano Fugazzi
Back cover picture by Antonio Caputo – Foto Anthony

Portions of this book previously appeared, in different form, in a number of publications.

First published in the United Kingdom in 2017 by lulu.com

ISBN 978-0-244-31897-0

Come writers and critics
Who prophesize with your pen
And keep your eyes wide
The chance won't come again
And don't speak too soon
For the wheel's still in spin
And there's no tellin' who that it's namin'
For the loser now will be later to win
For the times they are a-changin'

Come senators, congressmen
Please heed the call
Don't stand in the doorway
Don't block up the hall
For he that gets hurt
Will be he who has stalled
The battle outside ragin'
Will soon shake your windows and rattle your walls
For the times they are a-changin'

Bob Dylan, The Times They Are A-Changin' (1964)

CONTENTS

INTRODUCTION

2017 got off to a belting start. Just days after taking the reins at the Oval Office, President Donald J. Trump swiftly withdrew the United States from the Trans-Pacific Partnership and promised to tear up Obama's legacy, piece by piece.

Then the *fake news* saga erupted. President Trump forcefully shrugged off allegations linking him to the Kremlin.

According to the United States Intelligence Community, the Russian government interfered in the 2016 US presidential election as Russian President Vladimir Putin personally ordered an "influence campaign" to harm Clinton's electoral chances and "undermine public faith in the US democratic process."

Inquiries into the allegations followed on suspicions about possible links and financial ties between the Kremlin and Trump associates.

Trump labelled the entire affair as a hoax and launched a fierce attack against the press.

The extension of the southern border wall and the stance of the Trump administration on immigration also attracted a lot of criticism.

The claim that a combination of bad trade deals and mass influx of migrants into the US has caused a significant loss of jobs, particularly in the manufacturing sector, prompted me to fact-check Trump's words.

As documented in this book, both claims turned out to be factually incorrect. According to a study led by Michael Hicks and Srikant Devaraj of the Center for Business and Economic Research at Ball State University, 88 percent of jobs lost in the US manufacturing sector are actually due to productivity gains and changes to manufacturing employment. Additionally, a research by the Federal Reserve Bank of St. Louis shows that the relationship between unemployment and immigration is weak to nonexistent, even during periods of crisis.

It was Kim Jong-un, not the Mexican president, who put Trump's diplomatic skills to the test.

In April Trump said that he was sending an "armada" as a warning to North Korea. The move followed claims that Pyongyang had carried out a number of nuclear and missile tests.

It turned out that the aircraft carrier strike group he spoke of was actually heading in the opposite direction, away from the Korean peninsula.

Tension between the US and North Korea reached a new high in August, with Trump warning that any threats would be met with "fire and fury" and Pyongyang promptly announcing that it was "carefully examining" a plan to attack an American military base in the western Pacific.

In July Trump announced that the US would pull out of the Paris agreement on climate change. He said he decided to withdraw because the deal would hurt the American economy and US workers.

Trump has also taken a number of other steps that have alarmed environmentalists, such as approving the Dakota Access Pipeline project and rolling back over twenty environmental rules and regulations.

Even though Trump attracted a lot of criticism for his Berlusconi-esque antics, he somehow managed to establish a flock of fans abroad, particularly amongst the anti-establishment and no-euro parties.

French presidential candidate Marine Le Pen was hoping to follow Trump's slipstream and win the race to the Élysée Palace. However, sharing Trump's ideals on protectionism, anti-immigration and anti-establishment policies was simply not enough to win the presidential race.

A few miles north of Paris, UK Prime Minister Theresa May endured a torrid spring.

When a snap election was called on 18 April, May was sure to win a "strong and stable" mandate to kick start the Brexit negotiations.

But an almost certain overwhelming lead over the Labour Party evaporated over a matter of weeks.

At the June general elections, the incumbent Prime Minister failed to win a clear majority and was forced to join forces with the relatively unknown Democratic Unionist Party (DUP), a unionist political party in Northern Ireland.

Political uncertainty helped to destabilise the UK economy putting the Bank of England under pressure. Governor Mark Carney sent the markets mixed messages and made an extravagant U-turn on interest rates. At a speech at the Mansion House on 20 June, Carney made it very clear that "now is not yet the time" for a hike in interest rates. Eight days later, the Governor changed his mind and said a rate increase was on the cards.

Pressure is mounting on central banks to roll back their stimulus programmes to allow for more balance-sheet "policy space" in the future.

As a growing body of economic research claims that the monetary easing has increased income inequality, I reviewed a number of studies published during the year to back up this assertion.

With the Bank of England in the process of phasing-in the ring-fencing of banks from 2019, back in the US the Trump administration was also considering to enact a "21st century" version of the 1933 Glass-Steagall Act.

The 1933 law, which was repealed in 1999 by the Clinton administration, required the separation of consumer and investment banking.

However, Secretary of the Treasury Steven Mnuchin has softened Trump's initial stance since coming into office. "During the campaign we specifically came out and said we do support a 21st-century Glass-Steagall. That means there are aspects of it that we think may make sense, but we won't support a full separation of banks and investment banks," Mnuchin said at the Senate banking committee late in May.

Italy was in the news for calling on European countries to open their ports to migrant rescue ships. Italian authorities admitted to be struggling to cope with the growing influx of refugees from Africa.

Europe's worsening migrant crisis really puts the finger on the Continent's inability to act proactively when things are taking a turn for the worse.

The EU has a history of muddling through painful periodic crises. From agreements at the eleventh hour after months of squabbling with the Greek government to the rescue of Italy's rotten banking sector, the EU proved ineffective in dealing with the region's economic and social challenges.

Angela Merkel may have won a historic fourth term at the German federal elections. However, pressure is mounting on the Chancellor to restore what has been shattered, and what the Brexit vote has starkly reflected: there is no longer confidence amongst European citizens that a collective endeavour of solidarity and values can deliver what they need and want.

The times they are a-changin'.

TRUMPED-UP FACTS

Blame Bush, not Obama

President Bush's tax cuts and the military operations in Afghanistan and Iraq have contributed to the rise of the debt-to-GDP ratio to 105 percent.

15 January 2017 – When President Barack Obama took office in 2009, the United States were still coming to terms with the Great Recession. Since then, the state of the economy has improved significantly under President Obama's stewardship. The gross domestic product (GDP) has been growing each year since 2010, the unemployment rate has reduced to 4.7 percent in December 2016, down from the 10 percent recorded at the height of the financial crisis. Consumer confidence, private investments and the global competitiveness of the US economy have also returned to pre-crisis levels.

A high level review of the main economic indicators may suggest that Obama is leaving the White House on good terms and that the new US President, Donald Trump, will face fewer challenges in the first few months at the Oval Office than his predecessor did in 2009.

However, there is one indicator which may put under a different perspective – and, perhaps, taint – his legacy. A relentlessly rising public debt is likely to be a cause of concern and will unquestionably feature high on Trump's economic agenda.

Under president Obama the debt-to-GDP ratio has increased dramatically from 76 percent in 2008 to 105 percent.

One of the reasons for the increase is the introduction in 2010 of the Obama Care Plan, a healthcare law which was intended to increase health insurance quality and affordability, lower the uninsured rate by expanding insurance coverage and reduce the costs of healthcare.

Healthcare schemes such as Medicare and Medicaid are estimated to cost a total of $1.1 trillion. Pensions and other social security programmes aimed at providing financial security to the retired add another trillion to the public debt tally.

Although federal deficits and debt have been sharply higher under Obama, a Center on Budget and Policy Priorities report suggests that President Bush is largely to blame for the substantial deterioration in public finances.

President Bush's tax cuts, the military operations in Afghanistan and Iraq in addition to the aftermaths of the Great Recession contributed to the rise in the debt-to-GDP ratio as the Obama administration tried to revive the economy through a series of measures such as the Stimulus Package of 2009, tax-cuts, jobless benefits and financial industry bailouts.

The shifting balance of power

Trump's pledge to scrap America's international trade agreements signals the end of monetary easing and the return of fiscal policy.

31 January 2017 – Just days after taking the reins at the Oval Office, President Trump swiftly withdrew the United States from the Trans-Pacific Partnership (TPP), a deal which sought to establish a trade area between America and eleven other countries, including Australia, Japan and New Zealand.

During the presidential election campaign, Trump described the TPP as a "disaster done and pushed by special interests who want to rape our country."

Although the TTP had not been approved by Congress, several Asian countries had already put into place arrangements to smooth the introduction and implementation of the trade deal.

The US President signalled his intention to instead strike individual deals with the countries in the TPP, a group that represents about 13.5 percent of the global economy, according to World Bank figures.

Trump is also expected to start renegotiating the North American Free Trade Agreement (NAFTA), a deal which was negotiated by President George Bush and pushed through Congress by President Bill Clinton.

If NAFTA is set to be significantly reworked, or even dismantled altogether, the Transatlantic Trade and Investment Partnership (TTIP), a proposed trade agreement between the European Union and the United States, is likely to be postponed indefinitely.

"The election of Donald Trump seems likely to put our EU–US negotiations firmly in the freezer at least for a while," said Cecilia Malmström, the EU Trade Commissioner. "Yet, even if the US is our most important partner, and a necessary one, the world is bigger than one country. Trump or no Trump, we have a long list of many others willing to deal with the EU, and about 20 more trade deals already in the pipeline."

The rise of Trump and a renaissance of protectionism coincide not only with the demise of globalisation of trade but also with a shift in the balance of power.

Since the burst of the subprime bubble in 2007, a key feature of the Great Recession era has been the extension of the traditional role of central banks in managing financial crises.

For almost a decade the political establishment worked under the assumption that a lax monetary policy would have stimulated the economy.

Economic stimulus packages usually meant that central banks embarked on a quantitative easing (QE) programme, an unconventional form of monetary policy which creates new money to buy financial assets, typically government and corporate bonds, with the intention of favouring private sector spending in the economy.

Central banks around the world are said to be spending $200 billion a month on QE programmes, although this excess liquidity remains trapped into the banking system and is not lent out.

While monetary policies are partially to blame for failing to transmit liquidity to the real economy, local and supra-national governments are primarily to be held accountable for stepping back and delegating decision making powers to central banks and supervisory authorities.

The reintroduction of protectionist trade policies and the imposition of a 20 percent tax on Mexican imports, which is said to finance the completion of the US southern border wall, may appear anachronistic, particularly in the age of globalisation. However, it signals the return of fiscal policy as the only remaining macroeconomic tool available to decision makers.

As monetary policy has become less effective, this is the time for governments take bold decisions, addressing trade deficits and reviving local economies through the introduction of lower corporate tax rates to prevent delocalisation and loss of fiscal revenue.

Tariffs hurt the working class

A new study shows that US taxes on imported goods impose a heavier burden on lower-income households, women and single parents. Lower tariffs would have a considerably larger impact on poor households than the 2001 and 2003 tax cuts.

15 February 2017 – Economists often think of tariffs in a simplified way, as though they are applied uniformly to the economy, or targeted to protect only the most vulnerable sectors.

However, a new research by the University of California and the Council of Economic Advisers, an agency that advises the President of the United States on economic policy, suggests that taxes on imported goods impose a heavier burden on lower-income households, women and single parents.

The US collects more than $33 billion a year, corresponding to roughly 0.2 percent of GDP, in taxes on US imports.

A common argument in favour of trade protectionism is that increasing tariffs imposes a very small cost on many people to protect domestic industries.

Many policymakers overlook the fact that like any tax, the tariff burden does not fall uniformly across goods, but falls more heavily on particular goods and the populations that purchase them.

The burden is substantially higher for poor households than for the richest relative to their income.

The research shows that the poorest 10 percent to 20 percent of households in the income distribution pay about $95 a year due to tariffs, middle-income households pay roughly $190, and the richest 10 percent about $500.

The regressive effects of taxation are also observed across demographic groups as the tariff burden does not only affect lower incomes but is highest for women, single mothers and families with children.

Household	Tariff burden (% of income)	Tariff burden (% of expenditure, excluding mortgage, rent and utilities)
Married without children	0.34%	0.44%
Married with children	0.37%	0.53%
Single without children	0.37%	0.49%
Single parent	0.57%	0.69%

Table 1 – Tariffs across demographic groups

The average effective tariff on many categories of women's apparel exceeds that for men's apparel by a substantial margin. The effective tariff is 23 percent for women's versus 14 percent for men's on suits; 21 percent for women's versus 13 percent for men's on sweaters, shirts, and tops; 21 percent for women's versus 7 percent for men's on active sportswear; 15 percent for women's versus 10 percent for men's pants and shorts; and 13 percent on women's undergarments versus 7 percent on men's underwear.

Feminine hygiene products made of materials other than paper or cellulose are subject to tariffs ranging from 3.6 percent to 16 percent. The category, which includes both feminine hygiene products and nappies, has an average tariff of 7.6 percent.

The study also suggests that softening the tariff burden would have a considerably larger impact on poor households than the 2001 and 2003 tax cuts, which were estimated to boost the average income of a working-class household by $28 to $87 per year.

It is estimated that a 10 percent reduction in tariffs would increase the disposable income of low wage earners by $300 per year.

Why Trump can't blame trade for manufacturing job losses

Donald Trump claims that manufacturing jobs have left the US as a result of bad trade deals. However, nearly 90 percent of job losses are due to productivity gains and changes to manufacturing employment.

20 February 2017 – Just a few days after taking the reins at the Oval Office, President Trump pledged to make it easier for US automakers to invest in the country.

"We're bringing manufacturing back to the United States," Trump said. "We're reducing taxes very substantially and we're reducing unnecessary regulations."

President Trump also said that he would introduce a punitive tax to discourage US companies from moving jobs and factories overseas.

"A company that wants to fire all of its people in the United States, and build some factory someplace else, and then thinks that that product is going to just flow across the border into the United States – that's not going to happen," Trump said. "They're going to have a tax to pay, a border tax, substantial border tax."

Trump has hinted that the tax could be 35 percent to 45 percent of the value of the product.

Trump's words may suggest that competition from imports has decreased employment in the US manufacturing sector and therefore action is needed to protect jobs.

How US manufacturing jobs have changed since the 1960s

In 1960, about one in four American workers had a job in manufacturing. Today fewer than one in 10 are employed in the sector, according to government data.

Jobs in the US manufacturing actually increased in the years after the North America Free Trade Agreement (NAFTA) with Mexico and Canada went into effect in 1994.

However, the US has shed 5 million manufacturing jobs since 2000, a fact opponents of free trade mention often.

Productivity, not trade deals, the reason for a jobless recovery in US manufacturing

The US manufacturing sector was severely affected by the Great Recession of 2007-2009 and it took nearly seven years to recover to pre-crisis levels.

By 2014, the manufacturing economy had completely recovered with record levels of production.

Employment in manufacturing did not follow the same path of recovery as healthy growth in industrial production was not matched by a parallel increase in occupation.

According to a study led by Michael Hicks and Srikant Devaraj of the Center for Business and Economic Research at Ball State University, 88 percent of jobs lost in the US manufacturing sector are actually due to productivity gains and changes to manufacturing employment.

Growing demand for manufacturing goods in the US has offset some of those job losses, but the effect is modest, accounting for a 1.2 percent increase in jobs beyond what we would expect if consumer demand for domestically manufactured goods was flat.

The battle for energy domination

The Trump administration is set to reshape the geopolitical landscape of the energy industry by reducing reliance on oil imports and putting pressure on Saudi Arabia to reinvent OPEC by creating a brand new oil and gas cartel with America and the world's largest producers.

10 April 2017 – Donald Trump's plan to ditch Barack Obama's policy on climate change is part of a long-term plan which aims to create jobs and lower energy costs. The current administration is also hoping to reduce reliance on gas and oil imports and transform the United States into an energy exporting hub.

Trump's ambitious agenda is set to reshape the geopolitical landscape of the energy industry.

Energy Secretary Rick Perry recently said: "I don't want America just to be energy independent. I want America to be energy dominant."

The White House plans should not have come as a surprise. In December 2015 the US Congress lifted the trade restrictions on oil exports, a move which ended a policy introduced in 1975 in the middle of the energy crisis.

Plans to "make America energy dominant" are likely to result in the US challenging the Organization for Petroleum Exporting Countries (OPEC).

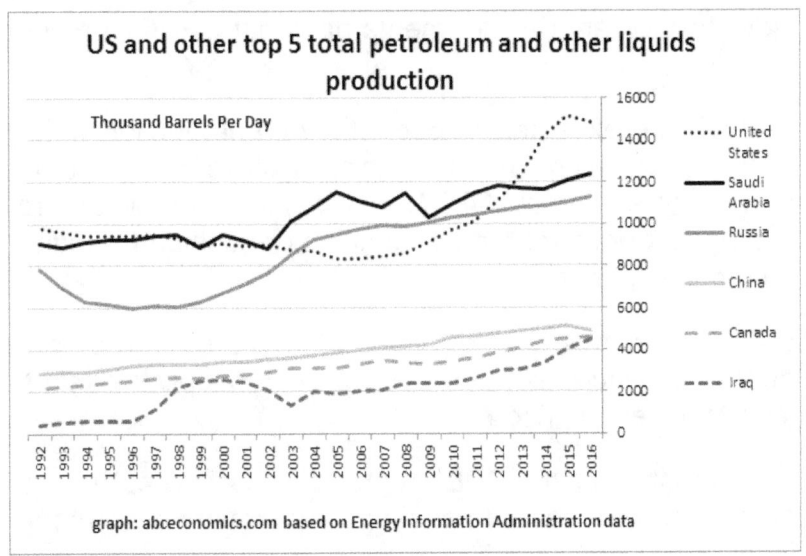

Figure 1 – US and other top 5 energy producers

OPEC is an intergovernmental body founded in 1960 and headquartered in Vienna. As of 2015, its 13 member countries accounted for 42 percent of global oil production.

Current members include Saudi Arabia (13 percent of world oil production), UAE (4 percent) and Qatar (2 percent) in addition to a string of countries America has been hostile to or at war with: Iraq (5 percent of global output), Iran (4 percent), Kuwait (3 percent), Venezuela (3 percent) and Libya (1 percent).

The main non-OPEC oil producers are Russia and the United States with a market share of 13 and 12 percent, respectively.

Until now OPEC has been the undisputed oil inventory and price setter.

However, recent developments have put OPEC in a tight corner.

The US are expected to boost their oil production with a view of becoming the single largest player. At the other end of the spectrum, OPEC has to choose between protecting its dominant market position or pushing for higher commodity prices.

If OPEC decides to retain its market share, then oil production will increase. However, excess supply is likely to lead to lower oil prices.

In December 2016, OPEC agreed to its first cut in production in eight years to sustain the recovery in commodity prices.

Early indications suggest that OPEC is likely to announce further cuts at the next meeting on 25 May.

OPEC's plans are in stark contrast to America's aggressive energy agenda.

Production of shale oil in the US is booming. The rate of growth is even faster than the first shale boom (July 2011-April 2015).

In 2015 member states of the oil cartel tried to put US shale producers out of business by flooding the market with cheap Brent oil.

However, US producers were able to readapt their operating model to lower oil prices. Additionally, the US decision to lift the ban on oil exports opened up new opportunities for shale producers.

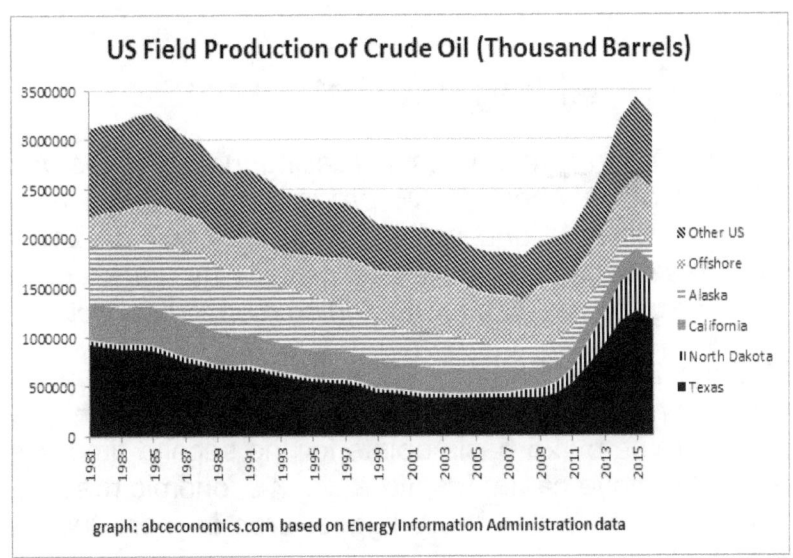

Figure 2 – Production of crude oil in the USA

OPEC members are desperate to put a floor under the price of crude oil. Their economies rely heavily on oil revenues to finance public spending.

Last year Saudi Arabia announced a number of unpopular austerity measures to curb spending. Other OPEC countries have also introduced tougher austerity measures to balance their books.

According to Bloomberg, the US may be able to raise production even faster if OPEC announces further output cuts. A zero-sum game which would irredeemably undermine OPEC's credibility in the global oil market.

Pressure would eventually mount on the Saudis to reinvent OPEC by creating a brand new oil and gas cartel with America and the world's largest oil producers.

Rising interest rates

The US Federal Reserve is increasing interest rates and planning to scale back its QE programme, despite weaker economic data and soft inflation numbers. St. Louis Fed President James Bullard explains why there are at least two good reasons for tightening monetary policy.

21 June 2017 – The US Federal Reserve pressed on with the normalisation of interest rate policy, by hiking interest rates by 25 basis points for the second time this year. The move came despite a weak economic reading. Retail sales recorded their biggest drop in more than a year in May.

The US Commerce Department reported that retail sales contracted by 0.3 percent last month, despite economists' predictions for a slight increase. Gasoline stations, department store and electronic shops took the biggest hit.

Sinking sales may be a sign of a continued struggle to compete with online retailers. Economists think that consumer spending will pick up in the second half of the year. Housing starts and building permits also declined in May.

Weaker economic data and soft inflation numbers are unlikely to shake the Fed's plan to increase rates again later in the year. The Fed is also said to be laying the groundwork for tightening monetary policy. The Fed is expected to unveil its strategy for reducing the size of its $4.5 trillion balance sheet by phasing out its QE programme.

At last week's Monetary Policy Committee, the Bank of England voted to keep interest rates unchanged at their record low of 25 basis point, and the QE programme remained capped at £435 billion, despite the surge in the rate of inflation to the highest level since mid-2013.

Although rates were left unchanged, surprisingly the Monetary Policy Committee voted 5-3 in favour of holding rates at their current levels. The vote's composition had been expected to be 7-1 in favour of a hold.

On Tuesday Bank of England Governor Mark Carney played down speculations that a rate hike was imminent. During his speech at the Mansion House, Carney made it very clear that "now is not yet the time" for a hike in interest rates.

"Given the mixed signals on consumer spending and business investment, and given the still subdued domestic inflationary pressures, in particular anaemic wage growth, now is not yet the time to begin that adjustment," Carney said.

"In the coming months, I would like to see the extent to which weaker consumption growth is offset by other components of demand, whether wages begin to firm, and more generally, how the economy reacts to the prospect of tighter financial conditions and the reality of Brexit negotiations."

Bank of England will have to eventually consider following the Fed's footsteps and start scaling back its QE programme.

In a recent article, St. Louis Fed President James Bullard explains why there are at least two good reasons for shrinking the central banks' balance sheets by rolling back QE.

One is that current monetary policy is distorting the yield curve.

"While actual and projected increases in the policy rate are putting upward pressure on short-term interest rates, maintaining a large balance sheet is putting downward pressure on medium- and long-term interest rates. A more natural way to normalise interest rates would be to allow all of them to increase together," Bullard said.

A second argument for ending reinvestments is to allow for more balance-sheet "policy space" in the future.

"The Fed should begin reducing the balance sheet now in case it needs to add to the balance sheet during a future recession.

"If, at that time, the policy rate is once again reduced to zero, the Fed may want to consider using QE again."

Trumping up new Glass-Steagall Act

In their 2016 manifesto, the Republicans vowed to reinstate the Glass-Steagall Act of 1933, which separated investment activities from retail banking. However, Trump appears to have backtracked on one of his key election promises.

24 July 2017 – In the midst of the 2016 presidential race, Donald Trump vowed to reintroduce the Glass-Steagall Act, a law put in place during the Great Depression. Democrat Hillary Clinton's husband, former president Bill Clinton, signed legislation in 1999 that repealed the Glass-Steagall Act.

In their manifesto, the Republican Party supported "reinstating the Glass-Steagall Act of 1933, which prohibits commercial banks from engaging in high-risk investment."

The Trump administration has softened initial plans to reinstate the 1933 law.

"During the campaign we specifically came out and said that we support a 21st century Glass-Steagall. That means there are aspects of it that we think may make sense, but we will not support a full separation of banks and investment banks," Secretary of the Treasury Mnuchin said at the Senate banking committee late in May.

Some critics, such as economist Joseph Stiglitz, have long seen the changes to Glass-Steagall as a major factor in the 2008 crash. By bringing "investment and commercial banks together, the investment bank culture came out on top," Stiglitz wrote in 2009. "There was a demand for the kind of high returns that could be obtained only through high leverage and big risk-taking."

Figure 3 – The original Glass-Steagall Act was introduced in 1933

US banking laws were comprehensively revised by the Dodd Frank Wall Street Reform and Consumer Protection Act in 2010 as a response to the financial crisis of 2008.

Even though many claim that the 1933 law would have limited the support that taxpayers provide to financial institutions in the form of deposit insurance and emergency loans from the Federal Reserve, the reality is that little would change should the Glass-Steagall Act be revived.

According to Bloomberg, "If a new Glass-Steagall went into effect today, institutions outside the Fed's safety net – such as money-market funds, investment banks and real estate investment trusts – would still rely on various types of short-term borrowing to finance more than $4 trillion in assets, or about three-quarters of all their holdings."

In the UK, the regulators are in the process of introducing the so called ring-fencing.

Under ring-fencing rules, which have become the UK's main regulatory response to the financial crisis, banks with more than £25 billion of deposits must hive off their consumer-facing business from riskier investment banking.

As it stands, only the five largest UK banking groups and some of their rapidly-expanding competitors will be in scope of the UK version of the Glass-Steagall Act when it comes into force on 1 January 2019.

Fake Chinese GDP

Sovereign states are no stranger to accounting controversies. This column reports on a number of alternative methods that can be used in measuring a country's Gross Domestic Product.

7 August 2017 – Creative accounting is a euphemism referring to accounting practices that may follow the letter of the rules of standard accounting practices, but deviate from the spirit of those rules.

The practice of overstating income and understating expenditure is usually associated with large corporation falsifying their financial statements. Enron, Wordcom and Parmalat are the most extreme examples of companies that cooked their books.

Sovereign states are also no stranger to accounting controversies.

In the late 1990s Greece falsified data about its public finances and deliberately obstructed the collection of accurate statistics to fulfil the Maastricht criteria and join the Eurozone.

In 2016 Ireland was criticised for its accounting practices as the country's Central Statistics Office claimed that the Irish economy grew by 26 percent in 2015.

More recently, attention turned to China. Many analysts are sceptical about the official statistics released by the Chinese government.

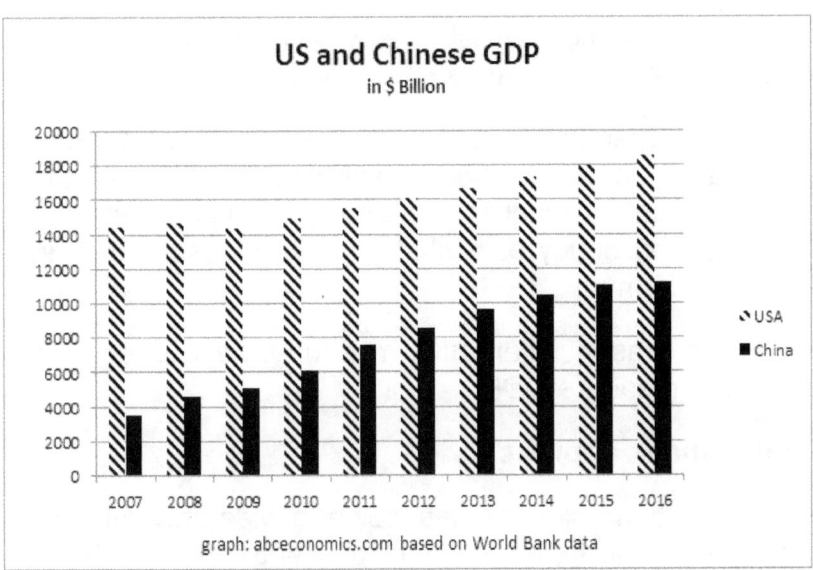

Figure 4 – Comparing United States and China by GDP

In a recent bulletin published by the Federal Reverse Bank of St. Louis, issues with official Chinese government statistics have fostered attempts to obtain better estimates of Chinese GDP, using a wide range of alternative methods.

Change in energy consumption

A method looks at variations in energy consumption. As an emerging economy with a large manufacturing sector, China consumes a lot of energy. Changes in energy consumption may be a good proxy for changes in economic output. Energy usage typically correlates with output and can be verified by third-party data.

According to economist Thomas Rawski, between 1997 and 2000 official figures reported that Chinese real GDP grew 24.7 percent whilst energy consumption decreased 12.8 percent during the same period.

Energy consumption is an imperfect proxy of economic growth. A country's energy usage could be impacted by several factors external to economic output such as increased efficiency or a shift from an industrial to a service economy.

For this reason, alternative measures have been developed to measure GDP.

Multi-index approach

Most multi-index measures look at a wide array of indicators, including freight volume, passenger travel, electricity output, construction indicators, purchasing managers indices, financial indicators like money supply and the stock market.

Unsurprisingly, all leading multi-index approaches suggest China's GDP growth is lower than the official estimates.

Li's index

Perhaps the most popular index for Chinese GDP is the one suggested by and named after Li Keqiang, then China's vice premier and now premier.

In 2007 Li Keqiang claimed that "Chinese GDP figures are man-made" and unreliable. The Chinese prime minister suggested using electricity production, rail cargo shipments and loan disbursements to estimate China's true economic performance.

Luminosity index

Another alternative method uses satellite data to measure the intensity of man-made night lights.

Unlike most economic indices, these data are immune to falsification or misinterpretation.

The night-lights data are gathered by Air Force satellites circling the earth 14 times a day. The satellites measure the light intensity emanating from specific geographic pixels, which can be aggregated to subnational, national and supranational levels.

In 2012, economists J. Vernon Henderson, Adam Storeygard and David N. Weil created a dataset using information from night-lights satellites and applied it to estimate GDP growth in countries with low-quality data. Their assessment suggests that between 1992 and 2006 the Chinese economy expanded by 57 percent whilst the official growth rate over the same period is about 122 percent.

Insight into North Korea

North Korea's economy grew at its fastest pace in 17 years in 2016 despite the isolated country facing international sanctions.

14 August 2017 – Take your typical small open economy with access to the world's largest single market and capable of attracting foreign investments and recording unprecedented levels of economic growth before 2008. Think of Ireland. Then think of the opposite. A closed, inward-looking, centralised economy. You must be thinking of North Korea, officially the Democratic People's Republic of Korea (DPRK), right?

You may have heard of North Korea's nuclear programme and their inclusion in America's Axis of Evil. However, chances are that you have never read anything about the state of health of their economy. Even the IMF does not hold any information on North Korea in their database.

Information is scarce and biased as Western media seem to be exclusively interested in reporting on the flamboyant management style of the country's supreme leader, Kim Jong-un. But never a word, or a true fact, on the economics of North Korea.

This column sheds some light on the state of their economy.

Circumnavigating sanctions against North Korea

Sanctions against North Korea have been imposed by various countries and international bodies. The current sanctions are largely concerned with North Korea's nuclear weapons programme and were imposed after its first nuclear test in 2006.

According to Ri Jong Ho, a former North Korean officer, sanctions against Pyongyang are ineffective because "there are too many ways around them."

Ri Jong Ho, whose job had been to raise money for the North Korean regime, said that he was able to circumnavigate the sanctions by simply handing a bag of cash to the captain of a ship leaving from the Chinese port city of Dalian, where he was based, to the North Korean port of Nampo, or by giving it to someone to take on the train across the border.

Russia and China are defying sanctions against North Korea

"Unless China, Russia and the United States cooperate fully to sanction North Korea, it will be impossible to hurt them," Ri said.

China's interest in North Korea is well known, but Russia's role is often overlooked. Amid calls for China to limit oil exports to North Korea, Russia has dramatically increased the amount of oil it has sent to North Korea this year. Some reports suggest that imports from Russia have quadrupled in recent months.

In the first half of 2017, China's trade with North Korea rose by more than 10 percent. The exports were largely driven by textile products and other traditional labour-intensive goods not included on the United Nations embargo list.

Sitting on a fortune of metals and minerals

North Korea has sizeable deposits of more than 200 different underground minerals, according to a recent report by Lloyd Vasey, founder of the Center for Strategic and International Studies think tank.

These include coal, iron ore, magnesite, gold ore, zinc ore, copper ore, limestone, molybdenite, graphite and tungsten, all with potential for the development of large-scale mines.

The country's magnesite reserves are the second largest in the world after China, and its tungsten deposits the planet's sixth largest, according to the report.

North Korea's mineral wealth was estimated at $10 trillion (£7.5 trillion) in 2012 by a South Korean research institute.

The North Korean economy is growing

According to the central bank of South Korea, the DPRK economy grew at its fastest pace in 17 years in 2016.

GDP in North Korea last year rose 3.9 percent from the previous year when the economy contracted due to low commodity prices.

Production in the agriculture, forestry and fishing sector rose by 2.5 percent in 2016 (-0.8 percent in 2015).

Mining production increased 8.4 percent in 2016 (-2.6 percent in 2015) boosted by an increase in the extraction of coal, zinc and other minerals.

Manufacturing output, which comprise both light and heavy industries, grew by 4.8 percent (-3.4 percent in 2015) mainly due to an increase in heavy chemical industry production.

Electricity, gas and water production expanded by 22.3 percent (-12.7 percent in 2015) mainly due to a rebound in hydroelectric and thermal power generation.

A 1.2 percent increase in the construction sector (+4.8 percent in 2015) was largely driven by growth in building construction and civil engineering.

Output in the services sector also expanded by 0.6 percent (+0.8 percent in 2013) mainly due to public investments in education and training.

DPRK GDP – Percentage change over previous year			
Sector (subsector)	2014	2015	2016
Agriculture, forestry & fishing	1.2	-0.8	2.5
Mining & manufacturing	1.1	-3.1	6.2
Mining	1.6	-2.6	8.4
Manufacturing	0.8	-3.4	4.8
(Light industry)	(1.5)	(-0.8)	(1.1)
(Heavy & chemical industry)	(0.5)	(-4.6)	(6.7)
Electricity, gas & water supply	-2.8	-12.7	22.3
Construction	1.4	4.8	1.2

Services	1.3	0.8	0.6
(Government)	(1.6)	(0.8)	(0.6)
(Other services)	(0.5)	(0.6)	(0.5)
Total GDP change	1.0	-1.1	3.9

Table 2 – North Korean GDP growth by sector

Gross national income and external trade

North Korean gross national income (nominal GNI) was valued at 36.4 trillion KRW, whilst GNI per capita stood at 1.461 million KRW in 2016.

The volume of North Korea's external trade (computed as the sum of exports and imports of goods, excluding trade between North and South Korea) totalled $6.55 billion in 2016 ($6.25 billion in 2015).

In 2016 exports increased by 4.6 percent mainly due to minerals and products of animal origin.

Imports grew by 4.8 percent year-on-year, an increase largely driven by machinery (+24.8 percent) and textiles (+20.5 percent).

Bilateral trade between North and South Korea

Bilateral trade between North and South Korea decreased by 87.7 percent year-on-year to $0.33 billion dollars in 2016. South-to-North trade volume shrunk drastically due to the shutdown of the Kaesong industrial complex.

US economy put at risk by climate change

A new study co-led by two UC Berkeley researchers estimates that the US economy could face a new recession if climate change is not stopped.

12 August 2017 – The poorest US counties are likely lose up to 20 percent of their incomes by the end of the century if no action is taken to combat climate change, according to a new research.

The study was led by two researchers from UC Berkeley, Solomon Hsiang, Chancellor's Associate Professor of Public Policy and principal investigator for the Global Policy Lab at the Goldman School of Public Policy; and James Rising, a Ciriacy-Wantrup Postdoctoral Fellow in Berkeley's Energy and Resources Group.

The study, which examines the economic consequences of climate change in the US, concludes that for every 1-degree Fahrenheit increase (approximately 0.5 degree Celsius) in global temperatures, the US economy could lose about 0.7 percent of its GDP.

The researchers used a flexible, high-resolution, county-by-county model that is based on the scale and structure of the country's population and economy in 2012.

They were able to calculate the impacts of a business-as-usual approach to climate change in the US through the end of the century, primarily reporting results for the benchmark period 2080-2099. They estimate their results' reliability at 90 percent.

The study suggests that climate change could lead to a severe economic downturn and increase income inequality.

"Climate change is going to be like a huge transfer of wealth from some people to others," said Hsiang. "This is kind of analogous to a tech boom in one region of the country and industry collapsing in another region. It is going to make the current economic cleavages in this country even bigger."

According to the study, rising sea levels caused by more frequent tropical cyclones will amplify storm tide heights and extend floodplains, worsening problems for low-lying coastal cities. The severe weather will inflict direct annual economic damages of 0.6 to 1.3 percent of GDP for South Carolina, Louisiana and Florida.

Climate change could affect agricultural yields in the Midwest as a result of rising global average surface temperatures.

Electricity demands will increase for all regions except the Rocky Mountains and Pacific Northwest, as rising demand due to hot days will more than offset falling demand from cool days.

The number of hours worked will decline about 0.11 percent for each additional degree in rising global average surface temperature for workers who are not generally exposed to outdoor temperatures, and by 0.53 percent for high-risk, outside workers. The high-risk employees account for about 23 percent of workers in sectors such as agriculture, construction, manufacturing and mining.

Annual national mortality rates will rise by roughly five deaths per 100,000 people for each degree Celsius increase in temperature.

Higher and higher temperatures in the South, which is already very hot, will cause climate change to take an even bigger toll in human lives in that region than in others.

Can climate change and finance work together?

The concept of a green economy has become a centre of policy debates. This column argues that the financial sector can contribute to fund private sector investment in the development of technological solutions to climate change.

20 August 2017 – In July Donald Trump announced that the US would pull out of the Paris agreement on climate change. He said he decided to withdraw because the deal would hurt the American economy and US workers.

Trump has also taken a number of other steps that have alarmed environmentalists, such as approving the Dakota Access Pipeline project and rolling back over twenty environmental rules and regulations.

The Paris climate agreement has been originally signed by 194 nations including China, India and the United States, the countries with three of the four largest greenhouse gas emissions.

The G20 countries account for more than 80 percent of global carbon dioxide emissions. Collective and decisive actions by the G20 and the implementation of the Paris agreement are key to establishing a sustainable and greener economy.

The Paris agreement aims to limit the increase in global average temperatures to well below 2°C above pre-industrial levels, the level beyond which scientists say we will see the worst extremes of global warming.

Many believe that the 2°C target is unachievable.

According to Schroders, the UK's largest-listed asset manager, global temperatures are on course to rise by up to 4°C, twice as far as safe levels.

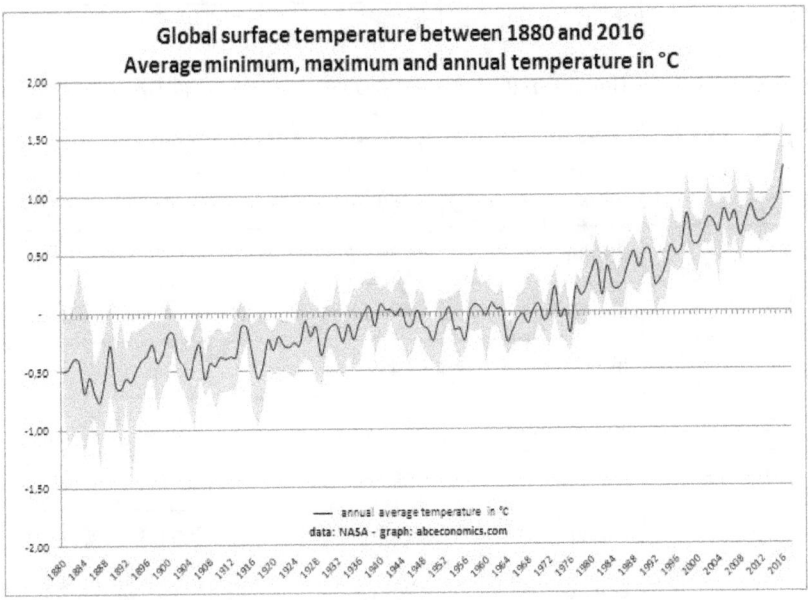

Figure 5 – The average surface temperature has increased from -0.5°C to +1.3°C.

The fund house, which manages $520bn for investors across the world, launched a tool to track climate change progress in July 2017.

The dashboard, which measures progress across political, industrial, technology and energy indicators, will provide a snapshot of likely temperature rises and help its fund managers to *evaluate the challenges ahead.*

43

2011 Total emissions	Country	Total Carbon Dioxide Emissions from the Consumption of Energy (Million Metric Tons)	Per Capita Carbon Dioxide Emissions (Metric Tons of Carbon Dioxide per Person)
1.	China	8715.31	6.52
2.	United States	5490.63	17.62
3.	Russia	1788.14	12.55
4.	India	1725.76	1.45
5.	Japan	1180.62	9.26
6.	Germany	748.49	9.19
7.	Iran	624.86	8.02
8.	South Korea	610.95	12.53
9.	Canada	552.56	16.24
10.	Saudi Arabia	513.53	19.65
11.	United Kingdom	496.80	7.92
12.	Brazil	475.41	2.41
13.	Mexico	462.29	4.07
14.	South Africa	461.57	9.42
15.	Indonesia	426.79	1.73
16.	Italy	400.94	6.57
17.	Australia	392.29	18.02
18.	France	374.33	5.73
19.	Spain	318.64	6.82

| 20. | Poland | 307.91 | 8.01 |

Table 3 – Emissions by country. Source: UCSUSA.org

Between 15 and 20 per cent of company cash flows are at risk, on average, because of climate change. "Global warming is a real problem, not just a societal one but a financial one," said Andy Howard, head of sustainable research at Schroders.

"Meeting global leaders' commitment to limit temperature rises to two degrees over pre-industrial levels means cutting greenhouse gas emissions per person by 80% by 2050, a period in which global incomes are set to triple."

Schroders is the latest big investor to voice its concerns about the impact of climate change on returns. Asset managers including BlackRock and Legal & General Investment Management have previously warned that investors should act to protect their portfolios from global warming.

The role of green finance

The impact of climate change on the economy has also attracted the attention of the Bank for International Settlements (BIS). In July 2017 the BIS hosted a conference on green finance.

Given the enormous investments needed to bring about a green transformation, the financial sector will have to play a central role in allocating resources towards a sustainable and green economy, the BIS said at the OMFIF conference in Frankfurt on 13 July 2017.

According to Luiz Awazu Pereira da Silva, the BIS deputy general manager, the transition to a green economy requires both governments and central banks to act together.

Governments and international organisations need to encourage a switch towards less carbon-intensive technologies through a combination of instruments, ranging from taxes and subsidies, to the introduction of more stringent environmental regulations and the development and deployment of information awareness programmes.

The BIS suggests that also central banks and banking regulators need to play a more active role.

The financial sector can contribute to fund private sector investment in the development of technological solutions to climate change.

"There are foreseeable benefits from adjusting to an economy with a smaller carbon footprint, where new policies and technology could cause a positive re-evaluation of a large range of asset classes," Luiz Awazu Pereira da Silva said at the OMFIF conference in July.

As green energy producers become growing sectors, there are also business opportunities associated with rising income and employment as substitutes for the traditional brown economy.

However, the green economy can successfully replace the conventional economic paradigm only with the help of governments and central banks, which need to actively support the growth and development of green finance through the issuance of instruments such as green bonds.

Green bonds were created to fund projects that have positive environmental and climate benefits.

The first green bond, the so-called "Climate Awareness Bond", was issued in June 2007 by the European Investment Bank.

Even though the total amount of outstanding green bonds has reached around $200 billion, they still account for only a very small proportion of financial flows (0.2 percent of the total number of bonds outstanding).

IMMIGRATION & INEQUALITY

Immigration is good for the economy

It is often argued that migrants displace native workers in the labour market and lower wages. However, newly published researches show that immigrant workers increase productivity and have no negative effects on unemployment and wages.

10 March 2017 – Immigration has been a hotly debated and politically charged topic. At the heart of this debate is the widespread belief by the general public and policy-makers that immigration has large effects on employment and wages.

A new study by the Federal Reserve Bank of St. Louis contradicts this assertion.

The research looks at wages and immigration figures for the years 2000, 2005 and 2010 to assess whether a change in immigration affects unemployment rates and payrolls.

The study shows that the relationship between unemployment and immigration is weak to non-existent, even during periods of crisis.

In some US states, an increase in the rate of unemployment is matched by a decrease in the proportion of foreign-born amongst the total population.

The research also finds no links between an increase in the proportion of immigrant workers and a reduction in hourly wages.

Changes in the level of wages are very similar across states even though changes in the proportion of foreign-born people vary a lot.

Immigration boosts productivity

While most studies assess the effect of immigrants on the labour market as a whole, a newly published research by the Centre d'Etudes Prospectives et d'Information Internationales (CEPII) looks at the issue from a different perspective.

The study analyses the impact of immigration on the productivity of French firms.

Between 1995 and 2005 France experienced a significant increase in the foreign-born population (from about 6 percent of the population in 1995 to 12 percent in 2005), consisting mainly of highly educated immigrants from other EU countries.

The researchers find that the employment of foreign-born workers has a positive effect on productivity.

Regions with a large increase in immigrant supply usually experience higher productivity growth, especially amongst firms that were initially less productive.

Central banks and inequality

Monetary policies are said to be a key driver of economic inequality. However, recent studies suggest that inequality is actually widening as a result of deep structural changes in our economy.

3 April 2017 – Widening income inequality has received a great deal of public attention and media coverage. In advanced economies, the gap between the rich and poor is at its highest level in decades whilst inequality trends have been more mixed in emerging and developing countries.

In the aftermath of the 2007-08 crisis, central banks took unprecedented steps to revive the ailing world economy.

Interest rates in a number of advanced economies have remained near zero since the financial crisis of 2008, and central banks have been pursuing unconventional monetary policies to fight economic recession.

One of the objectives of unconventional monetary policies has been to increase asset prices and money supply in order to boost consumption and economic activity.

Recent studies show that the transmission of liquidity shocks to the real economy has produced mixed results and increased inequality.

The linkages between monetary policy and the rise in income inequality have captured the attention of economists and international financial institutions like the Bank for International Settlement.

In a report published in March 2016, the BIS said that "while low interest rates and rising bond prices have had a negligible impact on wealth inequality, rising asset and equity prices have been a key driver of inequality."

Former chairman of the Federal Reserve, Ben Bernanke, strenuously defended the role played by the central banks in an article published in 2015.

"The claim that Fed policy has worsened inequality usually begins with the (correct) observation that monetary easing works in part by raising asset prices, like stock prices," Bernanke said. "However, widening inequality is a very long-term trend, one that has been decades in the making. The degree of inequality we see today is primarily the result of deep structural changes in our economy that have taken place over many years, including globalisation, technological progress, demographic trends, and institutional change in the labour market and elsewhere. By comparison to the influence of these long-term factors, the effects of monetary policy on inequality are almost certainly modest and transient."

A newly published study, led by professor Thomas Piketty, indirectly confirms Bernanke's assertions: income inequality is not affected by lax monetary policies.

According to Piketty, the bottom half of the wage earners in the US has been stagnant for decades.

From 1980 to 2014, average national income per adult grew by 61 percent in the US while the average pre-tax income of the bottom 50 percent of wage earners stagnated at about $16,000 per adult after adjusting for inflation.

In contrast, income skyrocketed at the top of the income distribution, rising 121 percent for the top 10 percent, 205 percent for the top 1 percent, and 636 percent for the top 0.001 percent.

The study concludes that rising income inequality in the US is largely due to excessive deregulation of industries and services, particularly within the financial sector, a tax system which has become less progressive, weakened unions and a chronically slow growth in the living standards of low- and moderate-income Americans.

Globalisation and income inequality

A newly published study says that world income inequality has increased within countries but decreased between countries.

17 July 2017 – Income inequality is a hotly debated topic and its cause is unclear.

Some argue that the gap between the rich and the poor has widened as a result of the monetary policies undertaken by central banks to boost consumption and economic activity in the aftermath of the 2007 financial crisis. Others believe that monetary policies have little to do with income inequality.

A newly published study, led by professor Daniel Waldenström of Paris School of Economics, observes global inequality, its trend between 1970 and 2015, and some evidence on its main drivers.

The research looks at data on earnings, taxes, working hours, and local prices for workers in 15 representative occupations since 1970, in up to 85 cities in 66 countries, in all the world's continents.

According to the study, global earnings inequality was very high in 1970 but has fallen to a lower level today. The main adjustment occurred in the early 2000s.

The reduction in the world's wage gap is largely due to earnings growth in Asia, which contributed to a drop in global earnings inequality.

Compared with earlier studies on global inequality in income or consumption, professor Waldenström has found that inequality in earnings and wages is slightly lower, but follows a similar trend.

Even though global inequality has somewhat reduced since the 1970s, the study suggests that the wage gap has increased within countries but decreased between countries.

"We find that within-country inequality rose over this period (by 5 Gini points), while between-country inequality fell (by 15 points), leading to the combined effect of a 10-point fall in total earnings inequality."

The study has also observed that inequality within occupations has fallen, especially in the trade and industrial sectors.

"This suggests that globalisation could be a potential driver of this earnings convergence trend," the researchers conclude.

How refugees and immigrants impact jobs

The recent surge in migration to Europe has brought new attention to economic research on the effects of immigration and refugee on natives' wages. Contrary to popular belief, immigration has no negative effects on employment.

10 September 2017 – Free movement of workers is one of the key rules governing the EU internal market.

Within the euro area, labour mobility plays a key role in adjusting imbalances in current accounts and local job markets.

A currency union eliminates exchange rate flexibility as a way of responding to economic crises. By allowing workers to move from regions hit by a negative shock to regions hit by a positive one, labour mobility could then work as a substitute.

The accession of ten new countries to the European Union in 2004 and the financial crisis of 2007-09 have changed the migration dynamics fundamentally.

Prior to the crisis, many citizens from Central and Eastern Europe migrated to Spain and other peripheral countries. The 2007-09 crisis profoundly impacted EU migration trends forcing many southern Europeans to relocate to Britain in search for jobs.

Immigration doesn't hurt native jobs or wages

The recent rise in UK immigration has ignited the debate on whether migrants affect local jobs and wages.

The stereotype of the Polish plumber, used widely as a symbol of cheap labour, encapsulates the commonly held belief that immigration in Britain has pushed down wages in the most affected jobs.

However, the balance of the research on this issue suggests that the share of immigrants in the workforce has had little or no impact on the pay rates of the indigenous population.

According to a Bank of England research published in December 2015, immigration may have a small negative impact on wages for some low-paid workers. But the idea that immigration is the main or even a moderately important driver of low pay is simply not supported by the available evidence.

A newly published study by the National Academies of Sciences, Engineering, and Medicine finds that the long-term impact of immigration on the wages and employment of native-born workers is very small, and that negative impacts are most likely to be found for prior immigrants or native-born high school dropouts. First-generation immigrants are more costly to governments than are the native-born, but the second generation are amongst the strongest fiscal and economic contributors in the US.

The US research also concludes that immigration has an overall positive impact on long-term economic growth.

Other researchers looked at the impact of refugees on local job markets.

There is a general consensus amongst researchers that refugee waves have little or no impact on native wages.

The large inflow of Cubans to Miami in 1980 did not affect native wages or unemployment; migration from Algeria to France after independence in 1962 caused a small increase in unemployment whilst the Balkan crisis of the 1990s did not materially increase unemployment in the refugee hosting countries.

AILING EUROPE

New Misery Index highlights Eurozone problems

A reformulation of the Misery Index exposes the growing disparities and imbalances within the Eurozone.

7 February 2017 – The Misery Index (MI) is an unofficial indicator of the state of an economy. Created by economist Arthur Okun, the MI is calculated by adding the unemployment rate to the annual inflation rate. An increase in the index is triggered by a movement in either variable, and means economic discomfort and negative consumer sentiment.

Politicians have found the index useful. George McGovern referred to the MI in scorning opponent Richard Nixon's economic record during the 1972 presidential campaign. Jimmy Carter used it against Gerald Ford in 1976. Ronald Reagan, who renamed it the 'Economic Misery Index', employed it in castigating Carter in 1980.

In 1999 Robert Barro, an economics professor at Harvard University, created his own version of the index calculated as the sum of the inflation, unemployment rates and the central bank's interest rate plus (minus) the shortfall (surplus) between the actual and trend rate of GDP growth.

In the late 2000s, Steve Hanke, an economist at the Johns Hopkins University, built upon Barro's MI and began applying it to countries beyond the United States. His modified index is calculated as the sum of the interest, inflation, and unemployment rates, minus the year-over-year percent change in per-capita GDP growth.

ABC Eurozone Misery Index

In 2014 ABC Economics, an independent think tank, refined the MI by taking into account government budget deficits and recalibrated the existing parameters to measure the economic performance of the euro area since the introduction of the single currency in 1999.

One of the most controversial aspects of the 2012 European Fiscal Compact, a stricter version of the Stability and Growth Pact, is a rule which requires general government budgets to be balanced or in surplus.

The ABC Economics iteration of the MI acknowledges net deficit positions and disregards surpluses.

As the ECB aims at inflation rates of 2 percent over the medium term, ABC Economics considered appropriate to include in the MI calculation the negative spread between a given country's inflation rate and the ECB target.

Additionally, the ABC Economics iteration ignores changes in interest rates as there is no rate differentiation within the single currency area.

Bearing in mind the above considerations on deficits, inflation and interest rates, the Eurozone MI will be calculated as follows:

ABC EZ Misery Index = unemployment rate + variation in GDP + ECB inflation rate gap + budget deficit + (interest rate − interest rate)

Although the MI is a function of lagging indicators, which reflect the economy's historical performance, recent trends in the euro area confirm that the index forms a close relationship with consumer confidence, a leading indicator, which often changes prior to large economic adjustments and, as such, can be used to predict future trends.

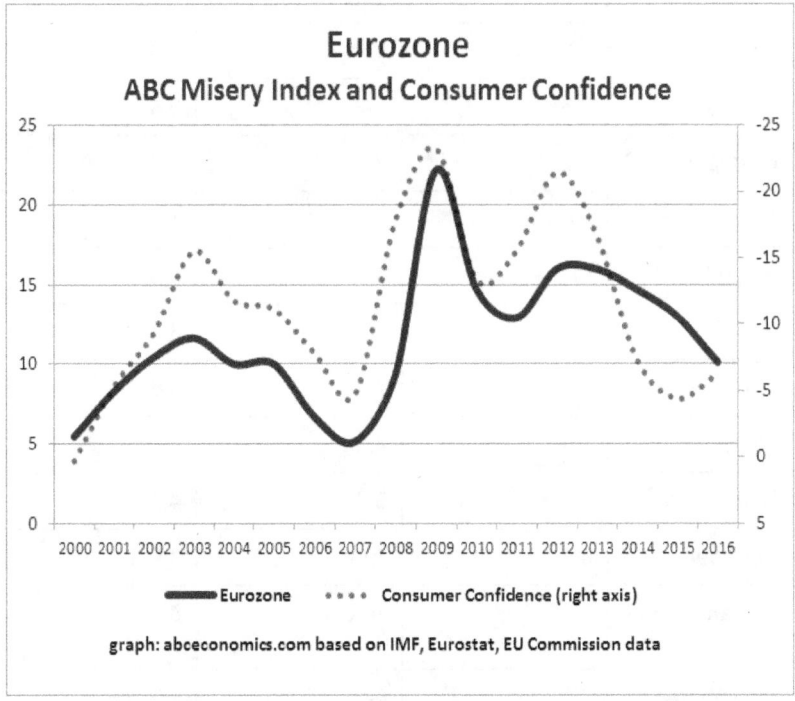

Figure 6 – Misery Index and Consumer Confidence (annual average value) in the Eurozone

The Eurozone MI provides clear evidence of growing disparities and imbalances within the monetary union.

Member States	2007	2016	2007-16 change
Eurozone	*5,1*	*10,1*	*5,0*
Austria	2,6	6,4	3,8
Belgium	4,7	8,9	4,2
Cyprus	-1,0	14,6	15,6
Finland	2,1	10	7,9
France	8,6	14	5,4
Germany	5,2	2,9	-2,3
Greece	11,6	30,4	18,8
Ireland	-0,9	4,6	5,5
Italy	6,2	15	8,8
Luxembourg	-4,2	2,4	6,6
Malta	6,4	4,3	-2,1
Netherlands	0,9	5,8	4,9
Portugal	8,5	12,4	3,9
Slovak Republic	2,6	10,6	8,0
Slovenia	-2,1	12,1	14,2
Spain	4,5	20,9	16,4

Table 4 – The evolution of the Misery Index in the Eurozone since the Great Recession. Excluding Estonia, Latvia and Lithuania.

From the introduction of the euro in 1999 to the collapse of Lehman Brothers in September 2008, the MI remained at moderate levels and did not differ much from country to country. However, the country-level MI started to diverge in 2008 in the wake of the Great Recession and was amplified by the mismanagement of the Eurozone sovereign debt crisis.

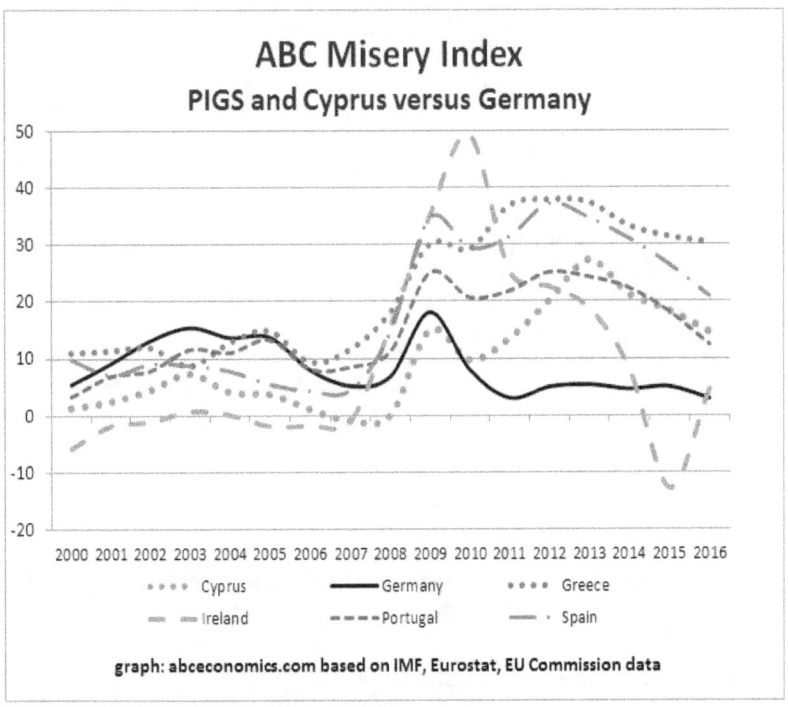

Figure 7 – Cyprus and 'PIGS' versus Germany

On average, the ABC Eurozone MI increased by 5 points between 2007 and 2016.

A country-level review of the MI suggests that only Germany and Malta are better off than they were a decade ago whilst amongst the periphery and key members of the Eurozone, the economic outlook deteriorated significantly, showing little overall improvement since the ECB has embarked on various forms of unconventional monetary policies.

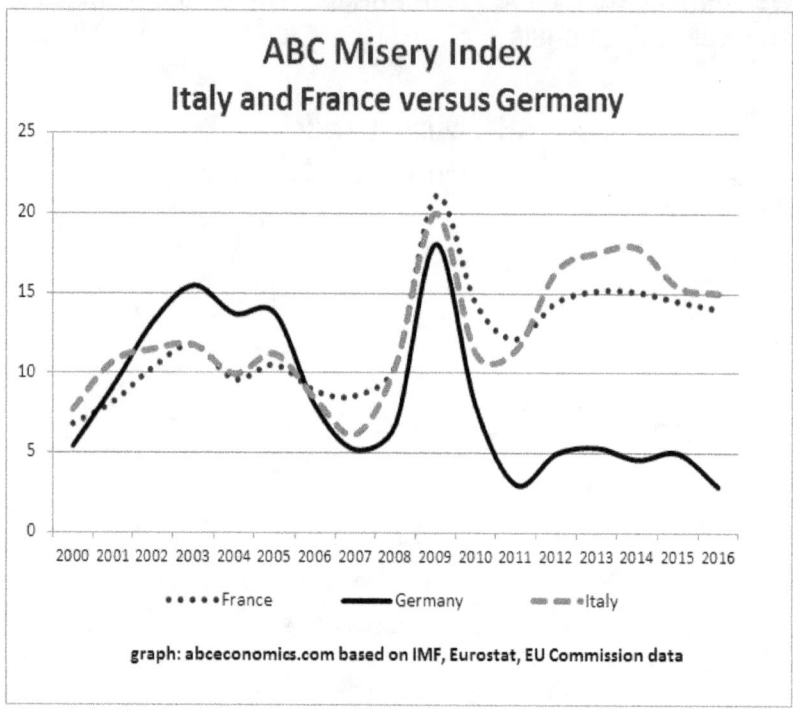

Figure 8 – France and Italy versus Germany

Populism booming in Europe amid cheap Chinese imports

A new research shows that European support for radical right parties is booming in regions most exposed to Chinese goods. Anti-globalisation and nationalistic sentiments are stronger amongst lower-income and less-educated Europeans.

27 February 2017 – The outcome of the Brexit referendum and the election of Donald Trump as president of the United States of America have fuelled a wave of anti-globalisation sentiment that could see several key elections won by right-wing populist parties.

France's Marine Le Pen and the Netherlands' Geert Wilders are all in with a fighting chance of winning power in coming months. Germany's anti-migrant party, Alternative für Deutschland, and Italy's Northern League are also gaining support.

In their political manifestos, nationalist and populist parties promise to protect voters from immigration and to toughen up trade defences against cheap imports.

Cheap Chinese imports and the increase in support for far right parties

According to a newly published study by the Milan-based Bocconi University, right-wing parties have made significant gains in regions most exposed to cheap imports from the Far East, particularly from China.

The researchers have studied the effects of Chinese imports on local employment and observed the electoral trends in 15 European countries, including France, Germany, Greece, Italy and the United Kingdom.

The study shows that stronger regional exposure to Chinese imports determines an increase in support for nationalist parties, a general shift to the right in the electorate, and an increase in support for radical right parties.

Support for radical right-wing populist parties is rising across Europe, particularly in regions where more workers were initially employed in those industries in which growth in imports from China was strongest – for example, textiles or electronic goods – and in years when the surge in Chinese imports in those industries was largest.

The demographics of right-wing populism

Last November the Bertelsmann Foundation, a German think-tank, published a survey research showing that Europeans are almost equally split when it comes to how they view globalisation.

A slight majority sees globalisation as an opportunity (55 per cent), while 45 per cent see it a threat.

The research shows that age, class, and education influence attitudes towards globalisation and cosmopolitanism.

47 per cent of those identifying themselves as working class say that they perceive globalisation as a threat versus only 37 per cent of middle class people.

37 per cent of respondents with high levels of education are less likely to see globalisation as a threat compared to 47 per cent of those with people with low level of education.

The Bertelsmann Foundation also finds that younger generations are slightly less fearful of globalisation (39 per cent of 18–25 year olds versus 47 per cent of 56–65 year olds).

The research ultimately shows that people who fear globalisation tend to support right wing populist parties.

78 per cent of Germany's Alternative für Deutschland voters, 76 per cent of France's Front National voters, 66 per cent of Italy's Northern League voters and 50 per cent of UKIP voters see globalisation as a threat.

Why leaving the euro is (im)possible

Article 50 of the Lisbon Treaty and the Vienna Convention allow a country to leave the Eurozone. However, the transition out of the euro could trigger mayhem and pose very serious economic and social challenges, at least in the short to medium term.

20 March 2017 – Debate over the future of the euro has gained traction since the burst of the Greek crisis in the aftermath of the 2007-08 recession.

Although most Europeans remain in favour of the single currency, anti-euro parties have made impressive electoral gains in a growing number of countries.

France's Marine Le Pen, Germany's anti-migrant party, Alternative für Deutschland, and Italy's Northern League share the same ambitious political agenda: if elected to power, they would lead their countries out of the Eurozone.

From a legal standpoint, a state member can withdraw from the Eurozone. The big question mark is how to go about it.

Euroexit is legally possible via Article 50 and Vienna Convention

An option would be to follow Britain's footsteps by triggering Article 50 of the Lisbon Treaty and commencing negotiations on the terms of the withdrawal.

A decision to leave the European Union would imply that a member state also intends to withdraw from the monetary union as the treaty does not feature a clause that allows a country to leave the Eurozone whilst retaining its EU membership.

The Lisbon Treaty makes it clear that the process of monetary union is intended to be "irreversible and irrevocable", a concept reiterated by Mario Draghi, the head of the ECB, on several occasions since 2011.

A government willing to leave the euro could consider other legal routes because the EU treaties do not make an explicit provision for leaving the currency union.

According to the Vienna Convention on the Law of Treaties, a state has the power to suspend or even withdraw from an international treaty even if the treaty does not state the latter.

Articles 61 and 62 of the Vienna Convention allow a country to justify withdrawal by fundamental changes in circumstances compared to those that prevailed at the time the treaty was ratified.

A country like Greece could argue that the evolution of the macroeconomic conditions has totally changed their balance between the advantages and disadvantages in their being part of the Eurozone.

Moreover, Article 44 of the Vienna Convention allows a state withdrawing from some clauses of a treaty while keeping the remainder.

As Denmark, Sweden and the United Kingdom have already opted-out from the euro, a member state could argue that the clauses of the EU treaty linked to the monetary union may be separated from the rest of the treaty.

There are some disputes over whether the Vienna Convention applies to EU treaties as not all member states, including France, have ratified it.

The medium-term challenges of leaving the euro

Although leaving the monetary union may be legally possible, the main challenge would be managing the transition from the euro to the revived domestic currency.

Under Article 50, negotiations between parties over trade and economic arrangements are expected to last two years.

However, a single currency member may run headlong into disagreements over a number of issues, including the resolution of the monetary union and the settlement of debts with Target2, the Eurozone's payments system.

"If a country were to leave the Eurosystem, its national central bank's claims on or liabilities to the ECB would need to be settled in full," Draghi said in January.

According to the latest data from Euro Crisis Monitor, Spain and Italy have amassed liabilities via the Target2 payment system of 339 and 376 billion euro, respectively.

Disputes over the settlement of Target2 claims and the disruptive effects likely to be caused by the disclosure of the plans to leave would bring any country on the brink of default.

Markets and investors would react very quickly to the news. Uncertainty over the future state of the economy would result into large capital outflows, an increase in bond yields, bank runs and loss of consumer and business confidence.

A step into the unknown that would pose more problems than solutions, at least in the short to medium term.

Frenkel's 7-step guide to Greek crisis

Argentinian economist Roberto Frenkel developed a 7-stage model to explain what happens when a weak country like Greece joins a currency union.

28 June 2017 – On 23rd June Moody's upgraded Greece's long-term rating to Caa2 and changed the economic outlook to positive from stable. Moody's said that the Greek economy started to show signs of recovery.

"Improved fiscal prospects on the back of 2016 fiscal outperformance, expected to lead soon to a reversal in the country's public debt ratio trend. The government posted a 2016 primary surplus of over 4 percent of GDP versus a target of 0.5 percent of GDP."

Moody's expects the public debt ratio to stabilise this year at 179 percent of GDP, and to decline from 2018 onwards, on the back of continued substantial primary surpluses.

Even though the near term outlook is brighter than it was anticipated only a few months ago, longer-term prospects remain challenging.

According to the European Commission, the need for additional debt measures should be assessed in a manner that caters for a number of downside risks.

"There is uncertainty surrounding the capacity of the Greek government to sustain high primary surpluses over several decades."

As public debt is expected to skyrocket to 241.4 percent of Greek GDP by 2060, the European Commission expects "significant downside risks to growth linked to aging populations and trends in total factor productivity."

Greece became the centre of Europe's debt crisis after Wall Street imploded in 2008, albeit most of the country's problems date back to the early 2000s.

Greece joined the single currency in January 2002 after failing to meet the EU's economic criteria in 1999.

According to Argentinian economist Roberto Frenkel, Greece's ill-fated decision to join the euro is the main cause of its current economic woes.

Frenkel claims that when a country with a weak economy adopts a strong currency, it would be only a matter of time before short term gains lead to long term pain.

Frenkel originally developed a 7-stage model to explain the 1998–2002 Argentine Great Depression, which culminated with the end of the peso's fixed exchange rate to the US dollar. However, this model has been since used to describe the current economic situation in Greece and the Eurozone's periphery.

Stage 1: Introduction of the single currency

The first stage of Frenkel's model begins with the introduction of a single currency, the euro, which shocked the national financial systems as it established stronger incentives for arbitraging between core and peripheral countries assets and led to the booming phase in the periphery of the Eurozone (Greece included).

Stage 2: Capital inflows and deregulation

The introduction of the euro, by increasing the incentives to international capital flows, generated renewed risks without a reinforcement in financial regulation. The educated reader may recall that Basel II came into force in 2008 when the EU regulators were still in the process of harmonising the capital markets.

Stage 3: High growth, low employment

At this stage, the combination of a fixed exchange rate, that is the single currency, and capital account liberalisation generated capital inflows, which expanded liquidity and credit within the Greek economy, fuelling the growth of financial and real asset sectors. As a result of these, output and employment growth accelerated.

Stage 4: Fuelling the bubble

In stage four, GDP and employment growth determined an increase in inflationary expectations and in the overall size of private and household debt.

Stage 5: External macroeconomic shock

During the fifth stage, an external macroeconomic shock – that is the burst of the subprime bubble in the US – brought the boom of the Greek property and lending markets to an end, causing many private enterprises to be rescued using taxpayers' money.

Stage 6: Austerity drags the economy

At this stage, the Greek government was forced to tighten its budget by promoting (or being asked to promote) austerity policies, which depressed the economy and led to the request of the so-called bailout programmes in 2010, 2012 and 2015.

Stage 7: Exiting the single currency

According to Frenkel, the cycle ends with a country leaving a monetary union. In Greece's case, this is an unlikely happy ending.

With the so-called Troika – the International Monetary Fund, the European Central Bank and the European Commission – owning most of Greece's debt, the Hellenic country's fate is determined by its creditors, not its people.

How Germany became an economic superpower

Labour reforms and a weaker currency helped Germany in building and keeping large current account surpluses even after the financial crisis.

12 July 2017 – Earlier this year, the Trump administration criticised Germany's enormous current account surplus. According to Trump's economic adviser, Peter Navarro, Germany is exploiting America and many other countries because it uses the euro, which is weaker today than the old Deutschmark would be. Thanks to a weaker currency, Germany is finding it easier to sell its cars and equipment abroad.

Germany and many other non-euro export-driven economies, including China, have been running current account surpluses since the early 2000s. During the financial crisis, external imbalances around the world began adjusting, and global imbalances started declining, with the exception of Germany, a country that kept increasing its current account surplus, even after the financial crisis.

What is a current account surplus?

The current account of a country measures the difference between its exports to and its imports from the rest of the world, and the international asset position of a country with the rest of the world.

If exports of a country are larger than its imports, then a country is likely to run a current account surplus.

In theory, the current account of all countries should sum to zero, since one country's exports is another country's imports. However, this is never the case.

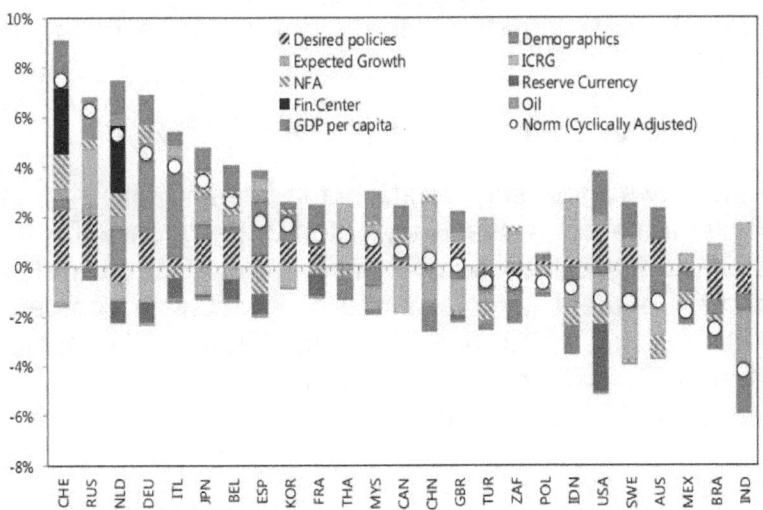

Figure 7. Estimated Current Account Norms and Main Components, 2016 1/
(percent of GDP)

Source: IMF Staff assessments.
1/ Norms are sorted from highest to lowest. Excludes Hong Kong SAR, Saudi Arabia and Singapore as they are not part of the EBA sample.

Figure 9 – Current accounts by component

According to the IMF, the world's current account balance does not net to zero for two reasons: time lags and creative accounting practices.

The euro is weaker than the old Deutschmark would be

Although the Trump administration blamed the German government of currency manipulation, the reality is that the euro is weak because of the ECB's accommodative monetary policies. The ECB Governor Mario Draghi is keeping low interest rates and buying bonds primarily to stimulate economies outside Germany.

Earlier this year, German Finance Minister Wolfgang Schäuble – a long-time critic of the ECB's current ultra-low interest rate policy – said that tighter monetary policy would help to reduce Germany's current account surplus.

Internal devaluation and Hartz labour reforms

Germany's trade surplus started increasing following the implementation of the Hartz reforms between 2003 and 2005. In 2002, the unemployment rate in Germany stood at 13.4 percent, after a period of low growth compared with the rest of Europe. The then German chancellor, Gerhard Schröder, asked Volkswagen's HR director, Peter Hartz, to lead a commission on reform in the labour market.

The Hartz reforms introduced new forms of employment, which helped in reducing wage growth and achieving near full occupation.

The labour reforms resulted in an internal devaluation of Germany inside the Eurozone, making German products more competitive. This increase in competitiveness led to an increase in exports, current account surpluses and a net credit Target2 balance.

One winner, many losers

Target2 balances are positions on the balance sheets of all euro area countries' national central banks. They reflect the financing of current account surpluses and deficits within the euro area.

As the euro is weaker today than the old Deutschmark would be, Germany runs a large current account position as well as a large credit in its Target2 balance.

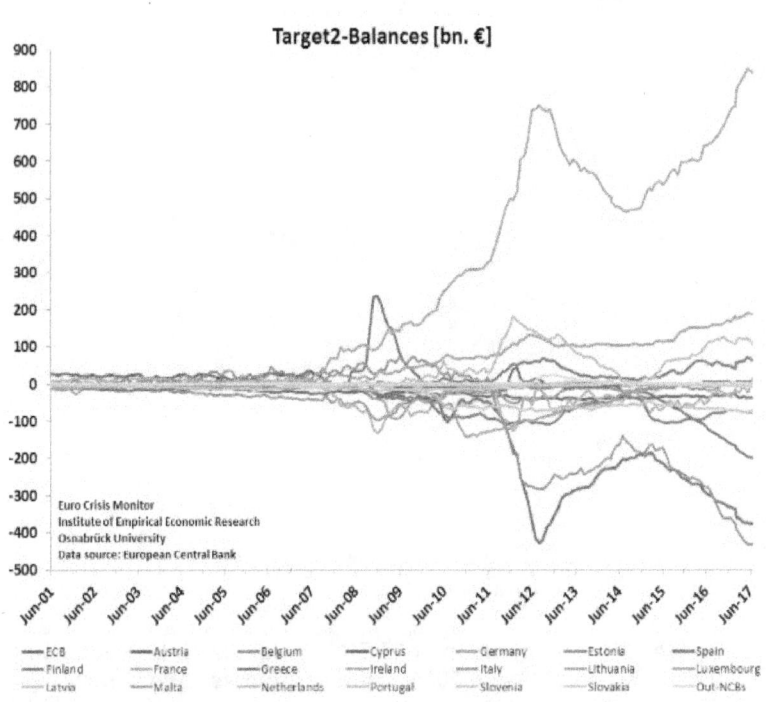

Figure 10 – The evolution of Target2 since 2001

Germany's net credit Target2 balance grew considerably in the aftermath of the 2007 financial crisis whilst many euro area members, braced for the economic consequences of the sovereign debt crisis, recorded high debit balances.

Movements in Effective Exchange Rates (EERs) highlight the growing imbalances within the Eurozone.

Nominal EERs are calculated as weighted averages of bilateral exchange rates. Real EERs (REERs) are the same weighted averages of bilateral exchange rates, adjusted for the effects of inflation.

James A. Caporaso and Min-hyung Kim

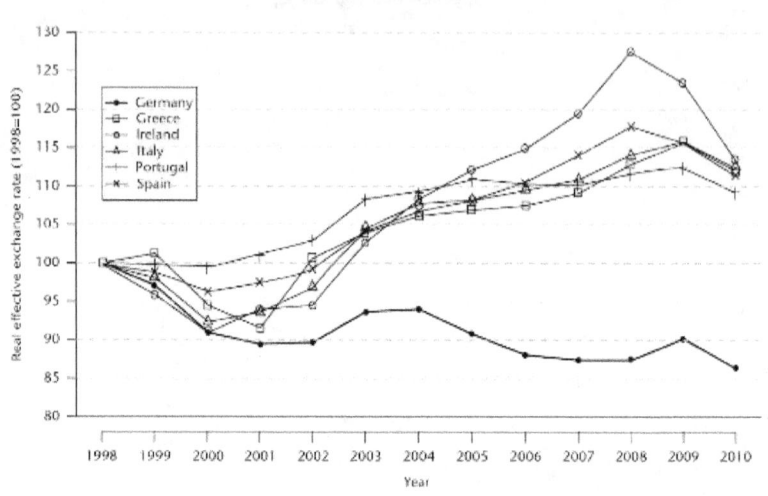

Figure 2.4 Real Effective Exchange Rate
Source: Eurostat

Figure 11 – The evolution of REER in a number of Eurozone countries between 1998 and 2010. Source: Caporaso and Min-hyung.

REERs are used for an array of purposes such as assessing the equilibrium value of a currency. They are measure of relative prices of goods as they are traded on international markets.

Absent currency differences, prices may vary as a result of different domestic inflation rates, wages and taxation.

A decrease in REER implies that exports become cheaper and imports become more expensive; therefore, a decrease indicates a gain in trade competitiveness.

Figure 11 shows the movement in REERs in a number of Eurozone countries compared to Germany.

Germany's REER decreased significantly in the first two years of the euro, with the index dropping from 100 to 91. These changes, which occurred before the Hartz reforms, suggest that Germany's exchange rate was overvalued.

Brexit putting 330,000 businesses at risk of insolvency

The number of businesses suffering "significant" levels of financial distress is increasing at the fastest rate in three years, a report has revealed.

31 July 2017 – New research from Begbies Traynor, the UK's leading independent business recovery practice, shows that 329,834 UK companies were experiencing "significant" financial distress at the end of June 2017, a 25 percent increase from last year.

The research showed that SMEs made up the majority of this increase (+26 percent) while large companies recorded a milder year-on-year movement (+12 percent).

"Our Red Flag research shows that a recent loss of momentum in the economy is putting increased financial pressure on UK businesses, with SMEs bearing the brunt of this rising distress, as businesses contend with uncertainty over Brexit negotiations and an inconclusive election result, alongside rising costs," said executive chairman Ric Traynor.

"These significant increases in financial distress also point to a slowdown in business investment at a time when the overall growth rate of the UK economy remains stubbornly sluggish."

Amongst the sectors facing the largest increases in financial distress, property and construction saw substantial rises of 32 percent and 22 percent, respectively.

"While we are seeing rising levels of distress across all corners of the UK economy, the quarterly deterioration in the property and construction sectors is particularly concerning, raising doubts over whether they have strong enough foundations to cope with upcoming headwinds, from Brexit and the rising cost of imported goods to the widening skills gap and its impact on labour cost inflation," Begbies Traynor warned.

The research also shows that the UK sectors most reliant on consumer spending have been hit particularly hard during the second quarter, with volumes of financial distress increasing year-on-year by 22 percent amongst leisure businesses, 17 percent for general retailers, 17 percent for automotive companies and 16 percent amongst bars and restaurants.

The report comes as the UK economy is showing signs of a slowdown. Preliminary numbers released at the end of July showed GDP growing at just 0.3 percent in the second quarter of 2017.

Brexit to put EU finances at risk

Britain's withdrawal from the EU could leave the remaining 27 countries with a €20bn a year hole in their budget, requiring additional EU taxes to fill the gap.

26 August 2017 – As a member of the European Union the United Kingdom makes payments or contributions to the EU. In return, the EU provides funding for various agricultural, social, economic development and competitiveness programmes.

The EU plans its spending over seven-year periods through the Multiannual Financial Framework (MFF).

Under the current MFF, which covers the years 2014-2020, the EU is planning to spend up to €960 billion over the period and make payments of €908 billion.

The EU's largest individual spending item is the direct payments it makes to farmers. Around a third of the budget is spent on farming subsidies.

The second largest spending area are the EU's programmes that help the least economically developed EU countries and regions to catch up with the other member states.

According to the European Commission, 69 percent of revenues in 2015 came from contributions made by its member states (69 percent in 2015), 13 percent from custom duties and sugar levies and 12 percent from value added taxes (VAT).

The remainder of the EU revenue in 2015 came from other sources such as interest on late payments, and fines on companies breaching competition law.

In 2016 the UK government paid £12 billion to the EU budget

In 2016, the UK's full membership fee was £17 billion. However, thanks to a deal negotiated by Margaret Thatcher in 1984, Britain gets a "rebate", an annual reduction in contributions. It is estimated that the rebate reduced the annual contribution by £5 billion.

According to the European Commission, in 2016 the UK was the second largest net contribution to the EU budget in absolute terms, and the third largest net contribution per head of population.

The UK will remain a member of the EU until its departure has been negotiated and will continue to contribute to the EU budget until it formally leaves.

Brexit divorce bill

The EU has been clear that when the UK leaves, it is expected to pay off its share of outstanding spending commitments and liabilities: this is referred to as the Brexit divorce bill or exit bill.

Estimates of the payment range from €25 billion to €100 billion.

The Financial Times in November 2016 originally reported that the European Commission was seeking an exit bill of €60 billion, based on comments by Michel Barnier, the EU's chief negotiator on Brexit. In February, the same author, writing for the Centre for European Reform

(CER), estimated that the bill could range from €25–73 billion. Bruegel, a European think tank that specialises in economics, has also given a similar range for the bill, at €25.4–65.1 billion.

Ultimately the one-off exit payment will be determined by the outcome of the exit negotiations.

	2011/12	2012/13	2013/14	2014/15	2015/16	2016/17
Custom du- ties and levies	2,205	2,171	2,200	2,263	2,314	3,020
VAT contribu- tions	2,276	2,398	2,163	2,316	2,751	2,477
GNI contribu- tion	11,218	12,303	13,845	14,154	12,570	11,440
Total contri- butions	**15,699**	**16,872**	**18,208**	**18,733**	**17,635**	**16,937**
Rebates	-3,516	-3,172	-4,130	-4,811	-4,068	-4,757
Gross con- tributions	**12,184**	**13,699**	**14,079**	**13,921**	**13,567**	**12,180**

Table 5 – UK contributions to the EU, £ million

A hole after Brexit?

Britain's withdrawal from the EU could leave the remaining 27 countries with a €20 billion a year hole in their budget, requiring additional EU taxes to fill the gap.

"With the departure of the United Kingdom, the rebate that was introduced as a concession to that country in the past will become obsolete," Günther Oettinger, the EU chief budget officer, said last spring.

According to sources close to the European Commission, the EU is evaluating a range of possible revenue-raising options, including the introduction of a tax on financial transactions (FTT).

Six years after the European Commission proposed an EU-wide FFT aimed at raising up to €30 billion per year, the bill remains on the table.

Germany, the highest net contributor, is reluctant to introduce a Robin Hood Tax as it is trying to lure financial services jobs to Frankfurt.

An alternative would be to increase contributions from the remaining 27 member states, albeit Germany and Austria have already made it clear that they do not intend to increase their share.

If revenues cannot be increased, then the EU officials may have to shrink the budget by reducing agricultural subsidies and economic development programmes.

Effects of terrorism on the economy

Federal Reserve Bank of St. Louis has published a study examining the effects of terrorism on trade, the economy and public spending.

29 August 2017 – Terrorism is the premeditated use of or threat to use violence to obtain a political or social objective through the intimidation of a large audience as well as the immediate victims. Acts of terror tend to have a harmful impact on the economy, with some sectors being more affected than others.

A recent paper by Bandyopadhyay, Sandler and Younas considers the effects of terrorism on trade. They find that terrorism tends to affect different sectors unevenly, with the greatest harm being experienced by manufacturing, compared with primary (non-manufactured) goods. Within manufacturing, they show that effects of terrorism are more damaging to high-skilled production than low-skilled production.

The specific target depends on the publicity that terrorist groups seek for their attacks. This publicity helps organised criminal activities advertise their strength and recruit sympathetic individuals who share their grievances.

If a terrorist group kills two people working in a shoe factory in Bangladesh, the attack is unlikely to attract international media attention. On the other hand, if two American tourists perish in an attack at an Indian hotel, the act of terror will receive much more media coverage.

Effects on the economy

Beyond the immediate loss of life and property, there are longer-term economic consequences stemming from terrorist attacks. If a country is perceived as particularly vulnerable to such attacks, foreign investors are more likely to refrain from investing in that country. By contrast, this can reduce the country's foreign direct investment (FDI), with a concomitant drop in employment opportunities.

Effects on bilateral trade

Recent high-profile terrorism attacks in France, Turkey, Belgium and Germany have raised concerns about the economic implications, not only within a targeted nation, but also amongst trading partners.

Bandyopadhyay, Sandler, and Younas find that nations that are more susceptible to terrorism are likely to import goods that are more subject to terrorism-related disruptions and to export other goods.

Terrorism can impact international trade through various channels. For instance, it can increase the costs of transportation by raising insurance premiums for goods shipped to higher-risk nations. Higher costs increase prices of imported goods, working effectively as import tariffs to reduce trade.

Terrorism can also lead to destruction of productive capacity of certain sectors of an economy, making these sectors more reliant on imports, which has the counterintuitive implication that terrorism may actually increase trade.

Bandyopadhyay, Sandler, and Younas also suggest that there is no reason to believe that terrorism necessarily reduces trade. While higher trading costs tend to reduce trade, changes in production patterns, as well as incomes of nations, can lead to general-equilibrium reallocations that can raise trade. Therefore, whether terrorism reduces or raises trade is a context-specific issue.

This finding partially contradicts earlier research. In 2004, Nitsch and Schumacher found that a doubling of terrorist attacks in trading partners cut their bilateral trade by almost 4 percent whilst other researchers recorded more modest effects.

Bandyopadhyay, Sandler, and Younas have also found that, while terrorism is necessarily welfare reducing for a nation that imports the greater terrorism-impacted good, the exporting nation may or may not be worse off because of potential gains from trade.

If a nation does not directly suffer from terrorist attacks, then it must gain (lose) due to terms-of-trade effects of terrorism if it is an exporter (importer) of the terrorism-disrupted good. In turn, this may make international coordination in counterterrorism policies more difficult to achieve because nations that gain from terrorism will have no incentive to participate in such an international coalition.

Insight into the Vatican Bank

A culture of secrecy and unorthodox accounting practices made the Vatican Bank one of the most notorious financial institutions. Pope Francis pledged to create a new era of transparency. This column looks at the Vatican Bank's latest set of financial accounts.

4 September 2017 – The world's largest unregulated bank is located in the heart of Rome and run by the Catholic Church.

The Istituto per le Opere di Religione (IOR), commonly known as the Vatican Bank, was established on 27 June 1942 by Papal Decree with the solemn duty to "serve the global mission of the Catholic Church by way of protecting and growing its customers' assets and providing them with dedicated worldwide payment services.

"In order to comply with this noble task that has been entrusted to the IOR by the Holy Father, the Institute must at all times ensure high-quality products and services, while assuring compliance with financial regulation."

Shadow banking out of the shadows

Unlike most financial institutions, the IOR does not cooperate with the Basel Committee on banking supervisory matters, nor complies with Basel III capital and liquidity adequacy requirements.

The Vatican Bank adheres to the Foreign Account Tax Compliance Act (FATCA), a United States federal law that requires US persons, including individuals who live outside the United States, to report their financial accounts held outside of the United States to the US Internal Revenue Service (IRS).

In 2016 the IOR agreed to exchange with the Italian authorities disclosures and client information for tax purposes.

All other forms of regulatory and governance oversight are independently carried out by the Holy See in accordance with the Canon Law.

Getting rid of dodgy customers

According to the IOR's latest set of published accounts, which were released in mid-June, the Vatican Bank's customers are active in the mission or perform charitable works at institutions such as schools, hospitals or refugee camps.

Other customers are institutional counterparties, employees and pensioners of the Vatican, religious organisations and dioceses.

The IOR does not formally take on individuals without a relationship to the Holy See as customers, nor does it accept corporate clients.

At the end of 2016, the IOR had 14,960 clients (14,801 in 2015), of which half (53 percent) were religious orders, 20 percent departments and entities of Canon Law, with the remainder split between clergy, parishes, Vatican employees and pensioners.

Since 2013 the IOR has closed down nearly 5,000 customer accounts under pressure from international anti-money laundering regulators concerned about its use as a tax haven. In addition, 2,600 dormant customer relationships were ended in 2013 and a further 4,600 accounts were lost in 2014.

Sometimes we can serve both God and Mammon

As at 31 December 2016, the Vatican Bank reported exposures in trading securities for EUR 2.5 billion (EUR 2.3 billion in 2015), mostly in sovereign and corporate bonds (96 percent), equities (3 percent) and investment funds (1 percent).

Additionally, the IOR recorded investments in precious metals totalling EUR 34 million, two thirds of which in gold bullion.

In 2016, the IOR's net profit was EUR 36.0 million (EUR 16.1 million in 2015). The year-on-year movement was largely attributable to higher income from trading activities coupled with a decline in administrative expenses.

The Vatican Bank's pension fund on a Highway to Hell?

According to the Vatican Bank's accounts, an actuarial loss of EUR 33 million was recorded in 2014, a deficit which brought the overall pension obligation liability to EUR 124 million. As at 31 December 2016 the total pension liability totalled EUR 121 million.

In August 2009 the Pope Emeritus, Benedict XVI, approved a pension reform bill increasing the retirement age to 67 and 72 for public servants and ecclesiastical personnel, respectively.

In July 2014 the Holy See unveiled plans to overhaul the IOR's pension fund "to ensure there are sufficient funds for future generations in a changing environment. In recent years, many Western countries – including the Vatican – have faced challenges in funding their pension system," the Holy See concluded.

BIBLIOGRAPHY

The following list indicates some of the sources consulted during the course of writing this book.

Academic research

Awazu Pereira da Silva, L. "Remarks at the conference organised by the BIS, OMFIF, the Deutsche Bundesbank and the World Bank Group", Frankfurt, 13 July 2017.

Baglioni, A.; Boitani, A.; Bordignon, M. "Is labor mobility a prerequisite for an optimal currency area?", Department of Economics and Finance, Università Cattolica del Sacro Cuore, 2013.

Bandyopadhyay, S.; Sandler T.; Younas, J. "Trade and Terrorism: A Disaggregated Approach." Working Paper No. 2016-001A, Federal Reserve Bank of St. Louis, February 2016.

Bandyopadhyay, S.; Sandler, T.; Younas, Javed. "Terrorism, Trade, and Welfare." Review, Vol 99, No. 3, Federal Reserve Bank of St. Louis, July 2017.

Basso, G.; Peri, G. "The Association between Immigration and Labor Market Outcomes in the United States." Discussion Paper No. 9436. Institute of Labor Economics (IZA), 2015.

Bräuninger, D. "The dynamics of migration in the euro area", Deutsche Bank Research, July 2014.

Caporaso, J.A.; Rhodes, M. "Political and Economic Dynamics of the Eurozone Crisis", Oxford University Press, 2016.

Clemens, M. A.; Hunt J. "The Labor Market Effects of Refugee Waves: Reconciling Conflicting Results", CEP Discussion Paper No. 1491, 2017.

Colantone, I.; Stanig P. (2017), "The Trade Origins of Economic Nationalism: Import Competition and Voting Behavior in Western Europe", BAFFI CAREFIN Centre Research Paper 2017-49, January 2017.

Colantone, I.; Stanig P. "Global Competition and Brexit", Baffi Carefin Centre Research Paper 2016-44, November 2016.

Colantone, I.; Stanig P. "Globalisation and Brexit", VoxEU, 23rd November 2016.

Enders, W.; Sandler, T. "Terrorism and Foreign Direct Investment in Spain and Greece." Kyklos, August 1996, 49(3), pp. 331-52.

Furman, J.; Russ, K.; Shambaugh, J. "US tariffs are an arbitrary and regressive tax." VOX, January 2017.

Hammar, O.; Waldenström D. "Global Earnings Inequality, 1970-2015", CEPR Discussion Paper 12019, 2017.

Hicks, M. J.; Devaraj, S. "The Myth and the Reality of Manufacturing in America." Ball State University Center for Business and Economic Research, 2015.

Hsiang, S.; Kopp, R.; Jina, A.; Rising, J.; Delgado, M.; Mohan, S.; Rasmussen, D.J.; Muir-Wood, R.; Wilson, P.; Oppenheimer, M.; Larsen, K.; Houser, T. "Estimating economic damage from climate change in the United States." Science 356: 1362-1369, 2017.

IMF Policy Paper, "2017 External Sector Report," July 2017.

Kawa, L. "Six Ways to Gauge How Fast China's Economy Is Actually Growing." Bloomberg, Nov. 2, 2015.

Keep M. "A guide to EU budget." House of Commons Library, Briefing Paper, Number 06455, 30 January 2017.

Keep M. "The UK's contribution to the EU budget." House of Commons Library, Briefing Paper, Number 7886, 8 August 2017.

Kilian, L. "The Impact of the Shale Oil Revolution on U.S. Oil and Gas Prices," Review of Environmental Economics and Policy, 10, Summer, 185-205, 2016.

Kilian, L., "How the Tight Oil Boom Has Changed Oil and Gasoline Markets," CEPR Discussion Paper 11876, forthcoming: Papeles de Energía, 2017.

Mitaritonna C, Orefice G.; Peri G.. "Immigration and firms' outcomes: Evidence from France", NBER, working paper 22852, 2016.

Moran, T. "Tariffs Hit Poor Americans Hardest." Peterson Institute for International Economics Real Time Economics Watch. (31 July 2014).

National Academies of Sciences, Engineering, and Medicine, "The Economic and Fiscal Consequences of Immigration", 2017.

Nickell, S.; Saleheen, J. "The impact of immigration on occupational wages: evidence from Britain", Bank of England, Staff Working Paper No. 574, December 2015.

Nitsch, V.; Schumacher, D. "Terrorism and International Trade: An Empirical Investigation." European Journal of Political Economy, June 2004, 20(2), pp. 423-33.

Piketty T.; Saez E.; Zucman G., "Distributional National Accounts: Methods and Estimates for the United States", NBER Working Paper 22945, 2016.

Rawski, T. G. "What Is Happening to China's GDP Statistics?" China Economic Review, Vol. 12, 2001, pp. 347-54.

United States International Trade Commission (USITC), "Harmonized Tariff Schedule", 2016.

Weidmann, J. "Remarks at the conference organised by the BIS, OMFIF, the Deutsche Bundesbank and the World Bank Group", Frankfurt, 13 July 2017.

Other sources

Bank for International Settlements; Bank of England; Bertelsmann Foundation; Bocconi University; Center for Business and Economic Research, Ball State University; Center for Strategic and International Studies; Council of Economic Advisers; Euro Crisis Monitor; European Central Bank; Federal Reserve; Federal Reserve Bank of St. Louis; Financial Times; House of Commons Library; Institute for Government; International Monetary Fund; Istituto per le Opere di Religione; Moody's; North Korean Economy Watch; Organization for Petroleum Exporting

Countries; Reuters; Schroders; The Economist; TREMR; University of California; VOX – CEPR's Policy Portal; Washington Post; White House; World Bank, Yahoo! Finance.